10307435

Like us on
Facebook

Visit us on the web at:
www.alta.lib.ia.us
or call (712) 200-1250
to renew your books!

5/18/16 Gumdrop Books $28.95

D1060322

Stephen Hillenburg and SpongeBob SquarePants

Stephen Hillenburg and SpongeBob SquarePants

Carla Mooney

San Diego, CA

© 2016 ReferencePoint Press, Inc.
Printed in the United States

For more information, contact:
ReferencePoint Press, Inc.
PO Box 27779
San Diego, CA 92198
www.ReferencePointPress.com

LIBRARY OF CONGRESS CATALOGING-IN-PUBLICATION DATA

Mooney, Carla, 1970-
   Stephen Hillenburg and SpongeBob SquarePants / by Carla Mooney.
      pages cm -- (Contemporary cartoon creators series)
   Includes bibliographical references and index.
   ISBN-13: 978-1-60152-866-7 (hardback)
   ISBN-10: 1-60152-866-3 (hardback)
   1. Hillenburg, Stephen--Juvenile literature. 2. Animators--United States--Biography--Juvenile
literature. I. Title.
   NC1766.U52H55 2015
   741.58092--dc23
   [B]
                                                                    2014047687

CONTENTS

Celebrating a Worldwide Icon

On July 17, 2009, Nickelodeon kicked off the Ultimate Sponge-Bob SpongeBash Weekend to celebrate the tenth anniversary of its beloved cartoon series, *SpongeBob SquarePants*. The network aired fifty hours of SpongeBob programming, hosted by Patchy the Pirate, a character who introduces many episodes of the cartoon show. The viewing event included an unprecedented eleven SpongeBob premieres and a top-ten countdown of celebrities' favorite *SpongeBob SquarePants* episodes.

In addition, Nickelodeon's sister cable channel, VH1, premiered *Square Roots: The Story of SpongeBob SquarePants*, the first full-length, original TV documentary about the long-running television series. The documentary tells the story of SpongeBob's path from cartoon character to international pop culture icon over a ten-year period. The hour-long documentary also features interview segments with the man who brought the character to life.

The Man Behind the Sponge

The creative genius behind *SpongeBob SquarePants* is Stephen Hillenburg, a former marine biologist with a passion for animation. Merging his love of the sea and cartoons, Hillenburg developed an underwater world, complete with a fun-loving sponge as a cartoon hero, and pitched the idea to executives at Nickelodeon. "Steve Hillenburg was a known entity—he had run [the network's animated series] 'Rocko's Modern Life'—we knew he was talented," says Marjorie Cohn, executive vice president of development and original programming for Nickelodeon. "The idea was fresh and funny and so well thought out it was hard to resist. But it was the delivery of the hilarious pilot that sealed the deal."[1]

When *SpongeBob SquarePants* premiered in 1999, its unique blend of humor and innocence attracted viewers. It took some time to catch on, but when it did, viewers were enchanted with SpongeBob and his friends under the sea. "For the first year or two we were on, no one really paid much attention to us. Then about the third year, we suddenly started seeing the show hit the radar and grow and become a part of pop culture, and that was another of those high-five moments," said Tom Kenny, the actor who is the voice of SpongeBob and his pet snail, Gary. Years later, the show continues to attract a legion of dedicated fans. "What I'm most proud of is that kids still really like it and care about it," Kenny emphasized in a 2009 interview. "They eagerly await new episodes. People who were young children when it started 10 years ago are still watching it and digging it and think it's funny. That's the loving cup for me."[2]

> "The idea [for a show about a sponge named SpongeBob] was fresh and funny and so well thought out it was hard to resist. But it was the delivery of the hilarious pilot that sealed the deal."[1]
>
> —Marjorie Cohn, executive vice president of development and original programming for Nickelodeon.

International Sensation

Since its debut *SpongeBob SquarePants* has become an international sensation. Between 1999 and 2009, the cartoon was the top-rated show for kids aged two to eleven. It consistently draws an average of 70 million viewers monthly and has generated billions of dollars in advertising, merchandising, and licensing deals. The show can even count the president of the United States as one of its fans. President Barack Obama says that SpongeBob is one of his favorite TV characters of all time, and he watches the show with his daughters.

For SpongeBob creator Hillenburg, the success of his cartoon is astounding. "It is a little much," he says. "I wanted to create something new and original. I figured we'd have a cult following for this weird little show. It still is a weird little show. It just got big. It's a big little weird show."[3] Kenny says that he thought the show would only last a year or two. "We did a seven-minute pilot, which we all thought was very funny, and that alone would have been enough of an accomplishment," says Kenny. "But because it was funny to us, we didn't know if anyone else would think so."[4]

An Innocent Sponge

Hillenburg says that retaining the innocence of childhood has always been an important theme for his show. In one episode titled "Grandma's Kisses," SpongeBob is embarrassed when his grandmother kisses him in public and his friends at work tease him, calling him a baby. He decides that he wants to grow up and tells Grandma that she cannot kiss him anymore. As an "adult," however, he misses the childhood pleasures of his grandmother's homemade chocolate chip cookies, bedtime stories, and sweaters made with love by hand. In the end SpongeBob realizes that he loves his grandmother's kisses and

Stephen Hillenburg, the creator of SpongeBob SquarePants, has long had a passion both for marine biology and animation. His two passions merged when he came up with a fun-loving sponge character and his quirky undersea world.

decides that he will never be embarrassed by them again, retaining his innocent, childlike point of view. "It's funny, but ultimately, I also think it's meaningful to have that point of view,"[5] Hillenburg says.

Many fans say that SpongeBob's eternal innocence has kept him in their hearts. "The show also came along at a time in the '90s when you had 'South Park' and 'Ren and Stimpy.' SpongeBob was much kinder," Kenny says. "He's always optimistic and I think people could relate to that. There's a yearning for positivity and kindness and a nicer, more appreciative, more inclusive approach to the world."[6] Fans agree that Hillenburg's SpongeBob keeps them watching and gives them a thirty-minute escape from the real world. "We were talking to some kids in upstate New York and asked them why they liked SpongeBob," says Julie Pistor, senior vice president of Nickelodeon Movies. "And this girl said, 'Because he's blissfully unaware.' And Steve said, 'That's exactly it.' For college students or any adult in a pressure-filled environment, you want to go back to your innocence sometimes. We'd all like to be blissfully unaware."[7]

The success of *SpongeBob SquarePants* did not happen overnight. Many people were responsible for the cartoon show's success, from artists to voice actors to network executives, all lending their talents and creativity to the show's production. At the start of it all was Stephen Hillenburg, the man who dreamed up the little yellow sponge and his underwater world.

CHAPTER ONE

Early Life and Career

Stephen McDannell Hillenburg's life began far from the sea. He was born in Fort Sill, Oklahoma, on August 21, 1961. Oklahoma is a landlocked state, centered in the middle of the country, far from the Pacific and Atlantic Oceans. Hillenburg's father worked as a draftsman and designer for aerospace companies, and his mother taught students with visual handicaps. Hillenburg also had a younger brother. While his brother followed his father's lead and became a draftsman and designer, Hillenburg says that he took after his mother's more artistic side of the family, especially his grandmother, who was a talented painter and artist.

In the mid-1960s, the Hillenburg family moved to Anaheim, California. If the Hillenburg family had stayed far from the ocean in Oklahoma, *SpongeBob SquarePants* may never have been created. In California the weather was warm and sunny for most of the year. There were also miles of beaches that lined the Pacific Ocean. On these beaches Hillenburg played as a child. There he developed an early love of the ocean and the amazing sea life it contained.

Inspired by Jacques-Yves Cousteau

As a boy Hillenburg watched several films and television shows made by the famous French oceanographer Jacques-Yves Cousteau. He was fascinated by Cousteau's work and says that watching Cousteau's shows got him interested at a young age in learning about the ocean and marine life. Cousteau was the twentieth century's most famous underwater explorer. In the 1950s Cousteau converted a British minesweeper vessel into an oceanographic research ship named the *Calypso*. He and his crew embarked on many research expeditions aboard the *Calypso*. They explored oceans all over the world.

Cousteau described his underwater research in a series of books. The most successful book, *The Silent World: A Story of Undersea Discovery and Adventure*, was published in 1953. Cousteau also made several films about the seas, the creatures that lived underwater, and his marine research. One of his films was a documentary based on *The Silent World*. This film won several awards, including an Academy Award in 1957.

Famed undersea explorer Jacques-Yves Cousteau explores the ocean depths. Cousteau inspired millions, including a young Hillenburg, with his underwater adventures.

On television, Cousteau inspired millions of people with his underwater adventures. In 1966 he made his first hour-long television special, *The World of Jacques-Yves Cousteau*. It premiered on the ABC television network. Then in 1968 Cousteau produced a documentary television series, *The Undersea World of Jacques Cousteau*. Millions of people, including young Hillenburg, watched each week as Cousteau and his crew on the *Calypso* sailed around the world and presented intimate studies of marine life and habitats. The series ran for nine seasons, from 1968 to 1976.

Cousteau's work inspired many young people to learn more about the ocean and its inhabitants. Craig McClain, the assistant director of science at the National Evolutionary Synthesis Center in Durham, North Carolina, credits Cousteau with inspiring him and a generation of young ocean lovers like Hillenburg. Says McClain:

> Growing up in a landlocked Southern state, in my youth I rarely visited the ocean, but I devoured every page of the 21-volume encyclopedia *The Ocean World of Jacques Cousteau*. Those books and Cousteau's television programs were staples of my childhood—my connection to the environment, to which I later dedicated my career. . . . Whenever anyone asks me what inspired me to become a marine biologist, I always begin my story with Jacques Cousteau.[8]

Like McClain, Hillenburg credits Jacques Cousteau with inspiring his interest in learning about life under the sea.

Learning About the Ocean

Along with watching Cousteau's ocean adventures, Hillenburg was able to explore the ocean regularly near his home in Southern California. In high school he checked out books from the library about diving, which often had only black-and-white photos of the sea. When he was fifteen years old, he snorkeled for the first time in Laguna Beach and was shocked at the colorful world he discovered. From that point on, Hillenburg was hooked on snorkeling and diving. He loved swimming underwater with the fish. He signed up for a free dive program at his high school, through which he obtained his certification in scuba diving. Spending time underwater also sparked a desire in him to learn more about life under the sea. He decided to study marine life in college.

After Hillenburg graduated from Savanna High School in Anaheim in the late 1970s, he enrolled at Humboldt State University. Humboldt State is located about 275 miles (443 km) north of San Francisco, in Arcata, California. The campus is near ancient redwood forests, mountains, and beaches, giving Hillenburg more natural spaces to explore.

At Humboldt State, Hillenburg studied marine life and natural resource planning. He says:

> Humboldt has incredibly rigorous science programs. It has dedicated teachers and students. Fortunately for me the school is not only surrounded by redwood forests, but it sits along an incredible part of the California coast. There are bays, estuaries, undeveloped coastline and open ocean and, of course, the school utilizes the availability of these resources in their courses. One time my biology class went into the mountains to collect stream organisms. We were collecting insects in this tiny stream and under this rock we found a 3-foot lamprey eel![9]

While at Humboldt State, Hillenburg also took art classes and says that he blossomed as a painter while at the school. Hillenburg remembers one of his art teachers at college asking why he was studying science when he was an artist. Some of Hillenburg's work was exhibited at local museums. In 1984 Hillenburg graduated from Humboldt State with a bachelor's degree in natural resource planning and interpretation, with an emphasis in marine resources.

Teaching Marine Biology

After graduation Hillenburg took a job teaching marine biology at the Orange County Marine Institute (known today as the Orange

County Ocean Institute) in Dana Point, California. Hillenburg recalls:

> As a kid, I was interested in art and painting and I was fascinated with marine biology. When I was about 15-years old I started scuba diving. The switch clicked and I decided I wanted to be a marine biologist, but I also liked being an artist. So I graduated from Humboldt State and my hope was to work in a national park on the coast. I eventually ended up working at the Orange County Marine Institute—which is now called the Ocean Institute. It was a great experience. I was a teacher there for three years.[10]

During his time at the institute, Hillenburg prepared exhibits and educated kids about marine science. The experience showed him firsthand how much children loved learning about the ocean and its creatures. "Working as a marine science educator, I had the chance to see how enamored kids are with undersea life, especially tide pool creatures. By combining this knowledge with my love for animation, I came up with Sponge-Bob SquarePants."[11]

One of Hillenburg's other jobs at the Marine Institute was dressing up and working as a "sailor" on the institute's tall ship, the *Pilgrim*. He dressed in costume as an 1830s seaman and taught children sailing work songs known as sea shanties. Hillenburg would have fun asking the kids, "Are ye ready, kids? I can't hear ye!" He would later use these phrases as part of the *SpongeBob SquarePants* theme song.

"As a kid, I was interested in art and painting and I was fascinated with marine biology."[10]

—*SpongeBob SquarePants* creator Stephen Hillenburg.

Making a Comic Book

While Hillenburg worked at the Ocean Institute, one of the educational directors noticed that he was talented at drawing. The coworker suggested that Hillenburg use his artistic talent to create a comic that could be used by the institute. Hillenburg agreed and wrote and illustrated a

While working at a Southern California marine institute, Hillenburg sometimes dressed up as a sailor who worked on the 1830s-era tall ship **Pilgrim** *(pictured during a 2011 festival). Part of his job included teaching sea shanties to children.*

comic book called *The Intertidal Zone*. The comic featured various forms of sea life, which he used to teach his students about the animal life in tidal pools. The comic starred sea creatures with human characteristics and featured Bob the Sponge as the cohost of the comic. He looked like an actual sea sponge and talked about sea life. Some of the other characters included a sea star and a shore crab. Many of the characters in this comic would develop later into characters on *SpongeBob SquarePants*.

Hillenburg approached several publishers to see if they were interested in professionally publishing the comic, but none accepted his work for publication. "I made this comic and I sent it out—and people liked it, but they didn't see how it would be a published item—you know, where they could make money from it. So I shelved the whole thing,"[12] he says.

Following Artistic Dreams

Even though he did not sell his comic, the experience of creating the animated book helped Hillenburg realize that he wanted to pursue his interest in art. While growing up in California, Hillenburg had always been interested in art, drawing, and cartoons. Like many children in the 1960s and 1970s, Hillenburg loved watching cartoons. Every week on television, cartoon characters starred in funny adventures that kept kids like Hillenburg laughing.

As a child Hillenburg also attended animation festivals and was fascinated by the cartoon films. He remembers, "In the '70s, as a kid, someone took me to a Tournee of Animation festival at the L.A. County Museum of Art. There, the foreign films—I was knocked out by that, especially [Dutch animator] Paul Driessen. His ["The Killing of an Egg"]. . . . That was the film that I thought was uniquely strange and that lodged itself in my head early on. I was interested in drawing my whole life."[13]

> "I made this comic and I sent it out—and people liked it, but they didn't see how it would be a published item—you know, where they could make money from it. So I shelved the whole thing."[12]
>
> —Stephen Hillenburg.

While working as a marine biologist at the Ocean Institute, Hillenburg continued attending animation festivals. Although he had enjoyed drawing and painting for most of his life, he says that he had not seriously considered pursuing it as a possible career. "Initially I think I assumed that if I went to school for art I would never have any way of making a living so I thought it might be smarter to keep art my passion and hobby and study something else," he said. "But by the time I got to the end of my undergrad work, I realized I should be in art."[14] The experience of working on the *The Intertidal Zone* comic book helped him realize that he wanted to pursue art as more than a hobby. "I was working at Ocean Institute—I was a marine biologist, but I was trying to figure out [how to get to] art school," he says. "It was at those festivals . . . that I thought: This is what I want to do. When I was at one of those shows, I saw several films . . . made at Cal Arts . . . and thought: That's where I should go."[15] So Hillenburg decided to go back to school, this time for art.

California Institute of the Arts

In 1989 twenty-eight-year-old Hillenburg left his job at the Ocean Institute. He applied to the MFA (master of fine arts) Program in

16

The Ocean Institute

The Ocean Institute is a community-based, nonprofit organization that is nationally known for its hands-on marine science, environmental and ocean education, and maritime history programs. The institute offers sixty-one award-winning marine science and maritime history programs for visitors. About 350,000 people, including K–12 students and teachers, participate in the institute's hands-on programs each year.

Located on 2.4 acres (1 ha) at the Dana Point Harbor on the Pacific Ocean, the institute is well suited for hands-on education about the sea. Students can voyage on the ocean, studying in labs and living on tall ships. They feel and taste the salty ocean water and examine live marine specimens. Whale-watch cruises take students to observe migrating whales. Other programs teach students how to collect scientific data and investigate the ocean world around them. Through its educational efforts, the institute aims to spark the curiosity of children and adults and inspire them to learn about the ocean. The institute also teaches the importance of ocean health and designs programs that help students understand and appreciate the connections between the ecosystems on land and under the sea.

Experimental Animation at the California Institute of the Arts (CalArts) in Valencia. For his application, Hillenburg had to submit a portfolio of artwork that included samples of his animation and visual work such as flip books, paintings, drawings, and storyboards.

CalArts has one of the top schools in the United States for aspiring animators and students in visual and performing arts—film, theater, art, dance, music, and writing. The school has churned out many famous and successful grads. Graduate Chris Buck won the 2014 Oscar for Best Animated Feature for his megahit film, *Frozen*. Other graduates include Chris Sanders, an Oscar nominee for the animated film *The Croods*; and Tim Burton, who is known for many films and animated features, including *The Nightmare Before Christmas* and *Frankenweenie*.

At CalArts Hillenburg would have access to one of the country's largest state-of-the-art animation laboratories. He would also participate in animation portfolio development workshops and learn from renowned visiting artists.

Experimental Animation Program

Hillenburg was accepted into the MFA program at CalArts that year to study experimental animation. At CalArts the Program in Experimental Animation has a well-known international reputation for excellence and innovation. The program's faculty, students, and alumni have won top awards at film festivals across the United States, Europe, and Asia. Graduates of this program are often credited with helping define animation as it is created today.

The CalArts experimental animation program gave Hillenburg a foundation to pursue his future animation projects. In this program Hillenburg learned a variety of animation techniques and concepts. He took courses in 2-D drawing and direct animation. He learned how to use stop-motion. He also worked with 2-D and 3-D computer-animation programs. In animation history classes he examined all forms of animation art. He says:

> I was in the experimental program where you actually learn every aspect of making a film, and there the idea was that you were the director and the creator of the project, that you would actually design and write and do all the editing and in some cases the music. . . . That was for me invaluable because I wasn't just studying how to be a character layout person for a commercial job. The hard facts are that in the industry, things are broken into jobs, and that experience helped me . . . to see the whole picture.[16]

After completing basic required courses, students in the experimental animation program work closely with CalArts faculty to create an individualized course of study. Students and faculty tailor coursework to each student's specific interests. Hillenburg worked with members of the school's faculty to develop and experiment with his own animation style and vision.

Working with Jules Engel

While a student at CalArts, Hillenburg met a teacher whom he says became one of the most significant influences on his artistic career—Jules Engel. Engel was a pioneer in the art of animation. He worked on Walt Disney classic animated films such as *Fantasia* and *Bambi* and created the well-known cartoon characters Mr. Magoo and Gerald McBoing-Boing. Engel was also internationally recognized for his abstract animation, live-action work, and fine art.

At CalArts Engel started the Character and Experimental Animation programs and served as the founding director of the Experimental Animation program. As a teacher, Engel valued the personal vision of each artist. He enjoyed helping his students develop and refine their own artistic vision. Engel also believed that other art forms had an influence on animation. He showed his students paintings

Jules Engel, an animation pioneer who worked on classic Disney animated films, including Bambi, *influenced Hillenburg's ideas about the art of animation. Hillenburg studied with Engel at California Institute of the Arts.*

Studying Environmental Management and Protection

Students who are interested in the relationship between humans and the environment, like Stephen Hillenburg, may choose to pursue a degree in environmental management and protection. Students who major in environmental management and protection use science to understand ecosystems and natural resources. They learn how humans interact with the natural environment. They build critical thinking skills to analyze, understand, manage, and improve the relationship among humans and the environment.

People with a degree in environmental management and protection work in several types of jobs. Some become environmental planners. Others work as environmental consultants, geospatial analysts, or environmental impact analysts. Others become environmental educators, outdoor recreation managers, park rangers, wilderness rangers, or restoration ecologists. In each of these roles, they work for the benefit of the environment and the humans that rely on it.

from world-renowned painters such as Pablo Picasso and Francis Bacon. He also shared the work of American modern dancers and choreographers Martha Graham and Mercier Philip "Merce" Cunningham with his students because he felt that studying movement was an important part of animation.

To help the next generation of animators, Engel established the Jules Engel Endowed Scholarship Fund at CalArts to support animator education. Director Mark Osborne, the creator of the 2008 animated film *Kung Fu Panda*, says:

Jules Engel was an amazing mentor to me and countless others. His enormous body of personal and professional work not only inspired us to be as prolific as he was, but inspired us to create with personal passion, no matter what the piece. He encouraged us to experiment, to follow our ideas wherever they would take us. Jules set a wonderful example for us to take chances and find our own voices, which is the most valuable thing for a filmmaker to have.[17]

Hillenburg studied with Engel and later talked about the influence the artist and educator had on his career when he was interviewed for a nonfiction feature film about Engel titled *Visualizing Art History: Experimental Animation and Its Mentor, Jules Engel*, which is still in production. Hillenburg said:

> Not only was Jules Engel a seminal figure in the history of animation, he also had a profound influence on countless generations of animators. He truly was the most influential artistic person in my life. I consider him my "Art Dad." *The work he produced both professionally and personally was groundbreaking. . . .*
>
> Jules always promoted the notion that animation could be a means of personal expression. Jules Engel's films are true examples of the unlimited possibility that the art form of animation offers.[18]

Hillenburg valued Engel's mentorship so much that he dedicated 2004's *The SpongeBob SquarePants Movie* to Engel, after his mentor died during the film's production.

Independent Animated Films

While a graduate student at CalArts, Hillenburg made several independent animated films. In 1991 he created *The Green Beret*. The film tells the story of a Girl Scout whose hands are so big and strong that she knocks down and destroys houses when she knocks on the door to sell her cookies. He also created a film titled *Animation Diary*, which consisted of 365 drawings, each drawn on the individual days that constituted the year 1991.

In 1992 Hillenburg made *Wormholes*, a six-minute animated film about the theory of relativity, for his graduate thesis production. He applied and received funding to make the film from the Princess Grace Foundation-USA, a nonprofit organization that assists emerging talent in theater, dance, and film arts by awarding grants, scholarships, apprenticeships, and fellowships. "It meant a lot," Hillenburg says. "They funded one of the projects I'm most proud of, even with SpongeBob. It provided me the opportunity just to make a film that was personal, and what I would call independent, and free of some of the commercial needs." He adds, "That was the one time I thought I could express myself as an individual and a person."[19] *Wormholes* was shown in several international animation festivals. At the Ottawa International Animation Festival in October 1992, it won the award for Best Concept.

In 1992 Hillenburg graduated from CalArts with his master of fine arts degree. The exposure of *Wormholes* at international animation festivals helped him land a job at Nickelodeon, a cable and satellite television network.

CHAPTER TWO

Working at Nickelodeon

After his graduation in 1992 from CalArts, Hillenburg took a job with Nickelodeon, a cable and satellite television network owned by the MTV Networks' Kids & Family Group, a division of Viacom. When it launched in 1979, Nickelodeon was full of commercial-free, educational programming. A show called *Going Great* featured five child prodigies in different fields. However, instead of being inspired, young viewers were lukewarm to the show. To better understand what child viewers wanted to see, network executives conducted a series of research meetings about kids and television in 1983. They discovered that kids did not really like the educational offerings currently on the air. Programs that featured extraordinary children who were good role models made everyday kids feel inadequate. "Adults love to see precocious children on television, because it's comforting to them," says Geraldine Laybourne, president of the network from 1980 to 1996. "But children don't find it comforting. We've learned from that."[20]

Focus on Kids

In the mid-1980s the struggling young network shifted strategies. It began to concentrate on developing programming that actually appealed to children. As a result, Nickelodeon began to develop more commercial shows such as *You Can't Do That on Television* and *Double Dare*. Launched in 1986 as Nickelodeon's first original program, *Double Dare* featured teams of kid competitors who answered quiz questions and competed in physical challenges. The contestants might have to throw enormous sausages into a huge frying pan held by a partner or race through an obstacle course filled with greased slides, piles of goop, and prizes for the winners. "Kids were mesmerized by it," Laybourne says. "It was pure play. We thought we'd captured lightning in a bottle."[21] This kid-centric focus quickly became the network's trademark.

Before long, children across the United States quickly recognized the orange, amoeba-shaped Nickelodeon logo. They cheered when Nickelodeon shows dumped green slime on young participants every day. They knew that Nickelodeon made television programming for them. By 1990 Nickelodeon had become the largest producer of

Model and actress Melanie Iglesias gets slimed on Nickelodeon's Double Dare *program in 2014.* Double Dare, *which began in 1986, was Nickelodeon's first original program.*

original children's programming. More children watched kid-focused shows on Nickelodeon than on the three major networks—ABC, CBS, and NBC—combined. Like its sister network, MTV, Nickelodeon featured flashy graphics and sophisticated programming. Its shows for kids aged six to sixteen featured gross humor, a sassy voice, and an attitude. "We try to elevate the status of kid-dom, to make kids feel important," said Laybourne in 1990. "Kids today feel insignificant. Our goal is not to educate them, but to entertain them, and make them feel good about being kids."[22]

At the same time, Nickelodeon faced some criticism from parents and other adults who felt that the network had gone too far in tailoring itself to kids, to the point that it was seen by some as being anti-parent and anti-adult. Peggy Charren, the founder of Action for Children's Television, a Boston advocacy group, said Nickelodeon promoted an aggressive attitude toward adults, with its characters portraying a wise-guy image that encouraged kids to be rude. Others, like Brian Sutton-Smith, a University of Pennsylvania psychology professor who specializes in studying children's play and serves as a consultant to Nickelodeon, disagrees. He said that Nickelodeon allowed children to have fun, noting that "kids are getting too domesticated. Nickelodeon's fumbling for it, but they're trying to set children's minds free with laughter, and that's something we don't see enough of."[23]

In 1990 Nickelodeon opened Nickelodeon Studios, a production facility at Universal Studios Florida. It filmed many of its live-action sitcoms and game shows at the facility. In 1991 Nickelodeon launched its first original animated shows—*Doug*, *Rugrats*, and *The Ren & Stimpy Show*. Previously, Nickelodeon had avoided producing a weekly animated show because of the high cost of quality animation. But, as Laybourne explained, the studio soon changed its mind. "We know that kids like animation, and that good quality animation lasts forever,"[24] she said in 1991. The three shows were successful and laid the groundwork for future Nickelodeon cartoons.

In 1996 Herb Scannell took over as head of the Nickelodeon network. Facing competition from Time Warner's Cartoon Network and the Fox Network for the kid audience, Scannell convinced Nickelodeon's parent company, Viacom, to invest in original animation.

The company agreed to spend $350 million and construct its own animation studio so that it could compete with animation giants Disney and Warner Brothers. "He bet his job on investment in original programming, and it paid off,"[25] says Michael J. Wolf, an entertainment industry consultant at Booz Allen Hamilton in New York.

Rocko's Modern Life

The success of Nickelodeon's first three original cartoon series led network executives to approve a fourth original cartoon series, *Rocko's Modern Life*. The show's creator was animator Joe Murray. When he was hiring for the new cartoon series, Murray saw some of Hillenburg's short films at the Ottawa International Animation Festival. Liking what he saw, Murray offered Hillenburg a job. Hillenburg describes the opportunity, saying, "After graduating, I had some films that were in festivals and I was invited to be a director on a show called *Rocko's Modern Life* by Joe Murray, who I learned a lot from about creating a show."[26]

Rocko's Modern Life was a cartoon that aired new episodes from 1993 to 1996 on Nickelodeon. The show followed the adventures of its title character, Rocko, an Australian wallaby. The style of *Rocko's Modern Life* was similar to the classic Warner Brothers cartoons, which heavily featured humor, sight gags, and good animation. The show was also full of adult humor, incorporating double entendre, innuendo, and satire in its script.

Hillenburg joined *Rocko's Modern Life* as writer and a storyboard artist. He quickly rose through the ranks, taking on more responsibility. He learned on the job about storyboarding and directing and says working on the series was a great educational experience. In the show's fourth season, Murray took a leave of absence from the show. Nickelodeon executives asked Hillenburg to step in and become the show's creative director. In this role, Hillenburg helped oversee the show's preproduction and post-

> "After graduating [from CalArts], I had some films that were in festivals and I was invited to be a director on a show called *Rocko's Modern Life* by Joe Murray, who I learned a lot from about creating a show."[26]
>
> —Stephen Hillenburg.

Storyboarding

Stephen Hillenburg got his start on Nickelodeon as a storyboard artist on *Rocko's Modern Life*. Storyboarding is a sequence of drawings that visually tell the story of an animation panel by panel. The process of storyboarding was developed at Walt Disney Productions in the 1920s and 1930s. A storyboard is like a large comic strip. It can be hand-drawn on paper or created digitally on a computer using software programs. The panels of a storyboard are arranged in the order they will appear in the story, film, or show. Each panel of a storyboard typically includes the characters in the scene. It shows where each character is in the scene and how they are moving. In some cases a storyboard can include what the characters are saying to each other or how much time has passed between storyboard panels. It can also show the perspective of the scene—whether it is a wide shot or a close-up.

Creating a storyboard helps a film's or show's directors visualize the scenes and find potential problems early in the process. With the entire story laid out visually before them, directors can organize and arrange the panels for the best effect before actual production and development begins. Using a storyboard can also spark new ideas that can be added to the story.

production operations. He also wrote scripts for the series and was the show's executive story editor.

Working on *Rocko's Modern Life* was an eye-opening experience for Hillenburg. He observed the multitude of problems that executive producer Murray had to deal with on a regular basis. "After watching Joe tear his hair out a lot, dealing with all the problems that came up, I thought I would never want to produce a show of my own,"[27] Hillenburg says. He had no desire to create his own cartoon show or run a show that others had created.

One day Hillenburg was directing an episode of *Rocko's Modern Life* titled "Fish and Chumps." Much of the story's action was set in the water. Hillenburg says that as he worked on the episode, it all came together for him—marine creatures, an ocean setting, and animation. He says that he began to see the possibility of merging his love of marine biology and animation.

Making Friends

While working on *Rocko's Modern Life*, Hillenburg met a group of people who later became central players in his vision of an underwater cartoon world, including Derek Drymon and Tom Kenny. Drymon would become the creative director on *SpongeBob SquarePants*. He remembers working with Hillenburg on *Rocko's Modern Life*:

> I met Steve at my first job in television animation on a show called *Rocko's Modern Life*. . . . [Steve] was a storyboard director, and I was a clean-up artist. *Rocko* was a storyboard-driven show, which meant the storyboard teams would work from an outline and would create the episode by drawing it out. Storyboarding was the best job you could imagine and I really wanted ed to do it, but I had no experience. I started self-publishing a comic book called *Funnytime Features* to show the show's creator, Joe Murray, what I could do. When Steve was promoted to creative director of *Rocko*, I was bumped up to storyboard artist largely based on what I did in my comic book.[28]

Kenny, who would later become the voice of SpongeBob, says that working as a voice actor on *Rocko's Modern Life* helped him learn how to do voice-over for animation. "*Rocko's Modern Life* was just one of those shows that were the first break for a lot of people who went on to do other stuff in the business," says Kenny. "A few years later, when Steve was ready to pitch a character of his own, he remembered me and thought I'd be good for his new character, SpongeBob."[29]

A New Cartoon Idea

While Hillenburg worked on *Rocko's Modern Life*, he began to imagine a new cartoon show, one that combined his love for the ocean with his love for animation. He explains how the idea for *SpongeBob SquarePants* first came to him:

> When I was working on *Rocko*, I had the comic book [*The Intertidal Zone*] in my office and one of the writers, Martin Olsen, walked in and said, "This is your show." It really wasn't—because it was an educational comic, but it started me thinking about animals that I liked—which are weird invertebrates and sea animals. I finally fused the two things I am passionate about together: art and marine biology and created a show that would eventually be called *SpongeBob SquarePants*.[30]

In 1996 Nickelodeon canceled *Rocko's Modern Life*. Hillenburg decided the time was right to pitch his idea for a new underwater cartoon to Nickelodeon executives. To develop his idea, Hillenburg recruited some friends and colleagues who had worked on *Rocko's Modern Life* with him. His team included creative director Derek Drymon, writer Tim Hill, and voice actors Tom Kenny and Doug Lawrence. In addition, Merriwether Williams, who had worked as a story editor on another Nickelodeon cartoon, joined Hillenburg's team.

Drymon remembers actively pursuing Hillenburg for the opportunity to write for this new show. He explains:

> Steve was starting to think about creating and pitching his own show. I remember his bringing it up to Mark [O'Hare, a storyboard artist on *Rocko's Modern Life*] in our office and asking him if he'd be interested in working on it. Mark had just sold a comic strip [*Citizen Dog*] to Universal Press Syndicate, and so wouldn't have the time. I was all ready to say yes to the offer but Steve didn't ask; he just left the room. I was pretty desperate to keep writing so I ran into the hall after him and basically begged him for the job He didn't jump at the chance. I had hardly any experience, and Steve and I didn't know each other very well, so I couldn't blame him. Of course, Steve was

never one to make a quick decision; he must have thought it over because he eventually offered me the job.[31]

Finding His Characters

When thinking about his own animated show, Hillenburg remembered how his young students at the Ocean Institute had been awed when learning about the creatures that lived in tide pools. Tide pools form on reefs, rocky shores, or beaches when the tide recedes. These pools of seawater can hold marine life such as sponges, octopi, crabs, and starfish. One day when driving on the Santa Monica Freeway on his way to the beach, Hillenburg says he realized that he had to use

While pondering an idea for his first animated show, Hillenburg thought about the marine institute's young visitors and their reactions to seeing the many creatures living in tide pools. At that point he decided that his show would feature some of these creatures as characters.

these creatures as the main characters in his new show. "I'd want creatures that wouldn't have been used," he says. "I knew a lot about tide-pool ecology. Those animals are the oddballs of the sea."[32]

For his main character, Hillenburg decided to draw a sea sponge, like those he had seen as a child and studied in school. "At first I drew a few natural sponges—amorphous shapes, blobs—which was the correct thing to do biologically as a marine science teacher," says Hillenburg. One day, though, he drew a square sponge that looked more like a yellow kitchen sponge than a realistic ocean creature. He realized that kids would identify more easily with the easy-to-recognize square sponge. "I think as far as cartoon language goes he was easier to recognize. He seemed to fit the character type I was looking for,"[33] he says. At first, Hillenburg named his sponge character SpongeBoy. Later he would change the character's name to SpongeBob. Drymon remembers:

> "He originally thought of the character as an amorphous shape, like a real sponge, but had hit upon a kitchen sponge shape, and I think that's when the character clicked in his head."[34]
>
> —Derek Drymon, creative director on *SpongeBob SquarePants*.

The first time Steve showed me a drawing of SpongeBob we were in his office. It was just a doodle in his sketchbook. I was really surprised to see that the character was a square; at the time it seemed like such an odd design idea. It really impressed me as something unique. He originally thought of the character as an amorphous shape, like a real sponge, but had hit upon a kitchen sponge shape, and I think that's when the character clicked in his head.[34]

Hillenburg says that viewers are drawn to sponges because they are odd and changing. He incorporated those characteristics into SpongeBob, making him able to re-form himself and change magically. He says, "I think the connection to SpongeBob is that sponges are the most elastic, changing, plastic creatures . . . and I wanted him to be able to do things that were really magical. So [SpongeBob] has these really creative moments when he can re-form himself." Hillenburg admits that SpongeBob's abilities are not typical of real-world ocean sponges. He explains, "Most sponges in the ocean are sedentary: They attach themselves to a rock and sit and filter-feed the rest of their lives, and reproduce, and that's about it. Not that they are not interesting, but they are not . . . mobile. They don't cook Krabbie Patties!"[35]

The end result of Hillenburg's character design was a yellow sponge named SpongeBob SquarePants. SpongeBob has a square, bright-yellow head. His eyes protrude as lidless balls, with three lashes. He also has two large front teeth and stick-skinny arms and legs. He wears a short-sleeved white shirt, a red necktie, brown shorts, white socks, and shiny black shoes.

An Underwater World

In addition to SpongeBob, Hillenburg created an entire cast of marine characters and an underwater world in which they could live, work, and have adventures. "One day it dawned on me that there was this whole environment under water, and I thought, what about a world that is steeped in all of this, but what if the characters act the way we do?" he says. He decided to populate this underwater world with a mixture of familiar beach town elements and surreal elements. "If you go to Hawaii and go to a gift shop you see pineapples for sale, and I thought it would be funny if there was a house that was a pineapple," he explains. Hillenburg imagined that living in a pineapple would be sweet-smelling and upbeat, the perfect place for an optimist like SpongeBob. "SpongeBob is an optimist, and I thought if anyone would live in one it would be him."[36]

The characters on *SpongeBob SquarePants* live in an underwater town called Bikini Bottom. SpongeBob lives in a pineapple house with his pet snail, Gary. He works at his dream job, a fry cook at the Krusty Krab restaurant, making Krabbie Patties. Hillenburg himself worked at a fast-food seafood restaurant while on summer trips to Maine with his family. He worked in the kitchen of a dockside restaurant for a boss who was a former army cook. Hillenburg says that he used his experiences at the restaurant and his boss to create details for the Krusty Krab and the character of Mr. Krabs.

SpongeBob's neighbor and best friend is Patrick Star, a dimwitted but lovable pink starfish. Another friend, Sandy Cheeks, is a

Hillenburg created a whole array of quirky underwater characters. In addition to SpongeBob—the square yellow sponge with lidless eyes and skinny arms and legs—is his best friend Patrick, a dim-witted but lovable pink sea star.

squirrel from Texas that lives in an oxygen-filled sea dome. Always a thrill seeker, Sandy accepted a challenge to live under the sea. Other characters include Squidward Tentacles, a sour squid who lives next door to SpongeBob and works with him at the Krusty Krab restaurant. Squidward's negative attitude is the opposite of SpongeBob's optimism, and he is often annoyed with the antics of SpongeBob and

Patrick. Another resident of Bikini Bottom is Mr. Krabs, a greedy red crab who owns the Krusty Krab restaurant and is SpongeBob's boss. Mr. Krabs spends his day counting money and trying to increase sales at the restaurant.

The villain of the show is Plankton. A little guy with big plans, Plankton owns a rival restaurant in Bikini Bottom called the Chum Bucket. He constantly devises plans to steal Krusty Krab's customers and, ultimately, the secret recipe for Krusty Krab's famous Krabbie Patty.

Although each of the show's characters is based on an actual animal species, their cartoon forms hold little similarity to real sponges, crabs, or other marine animals. Hillenburg explains that when creating the characters in Bikini Bottom, he did not intend to make them scientifically accurate. His main purpose was to entertain kids, not to teach science with the show.

Tom Kenny, who is the voice of SpongeBob, says that Hillenburg was incredibly detailed in his ideas for the new show. Kenny remembers Hillenburg asking him to look at his work, and Kenny was impressed at how well thought-out and conceived Hillenburg's initial plans were. "There were character drawings—not really model sheets—but drawings of the characters, personality profiles, graphic studies of SpongeBob's pineapple house and Squidward's tiki-head house, the Krusty Krab, a lobster-trap-shaped structure. It was typical Steve: fully realized before he even mentioned it to anyone. By the time I saw it, I was just blown away by the groundwork,"[37] says Kenny.

Child-Friendly Innocence

Many popular cartoons in the 1990s like *Ren & Stimpy*, *The Simpsons*, and *Beavis and Butt-Head* featured sarcastic characters and adult-themed humor. Hillenburg followed a different path when creating SpongeBob and the underwater world of Bikini Bottom. Instead of being crass or flippant, SpongeBob is naive and sincere. Hillenburg wanted SpongeBob to have a young, boyish attitude. He says the classic personas of comedic actors Jerry Lewis, Pee-Wee Herman, and Stan Laurel were inspirations for this character. He wanted Sponge-Bob to capture their innocent, kid-like humor. "There is something kind of unique about this," explains Robert Thompson, a professor of

The Voice Behind SpongeBob

Growing up in Syracuse, New York, Tom Kenny had no idea that one day he would be the voice behind one of the world's most famous cartoon characters. From an early age, however, Kenny loved performing, and like many children, he loved cartoons. In grade school he wrote and drew his own comic strips and acted out comedy skits. In high school he began performing stand-up comedy routines with friends. After several years of performing in comedy clubs, Kenny eventually realized that stand-up was not where his talents were.

Kenny's first break into voice acting came on Nickelodeon's cartoon series, *Rocko's Modern Life.* He says that from the first moment he stood behind the microphone, he felt comfortable. Kenny's work on *Rocko's Modern Life* introduced him to Stephen Hillenburg, who also worked on the show. When Hillenburg came up with his idea for a new underwater cartoon, he asked Kenny for his voice. Hillenburg remembered a voice that Kenny had used for a minor character in *Rocko's Modern Life* and wanted a similar voice.

Kenny says doing voice-over is more than reading out loud in a funny voice. "Really, it's about inhabiting a world and a character and having fun with it. It's like any other acting in that you get in that zone and be that character," he says. "On every show, I just try to figure out how to be as effective as possible and further the creator's vision because it's their show, it's their baby."

Quoted in Jenelle Riley, "Tom Kenny Finds His Voice as SpongeBob SquarePants," Backstage, April 27, 2011. www.backstage.com.

communications and director of the Center for the Study of Popular Television at Syracuse University. "It seems to be a refreshing breath from the pre-irony era. There's no sense of the elbow-in-rib, tongue-in-cheek aesthetic that so permeates the rest of American culture."[38]

Additionally, in every adventure in Bikini Bottom, Hillenburg chose not to include any references to drug use, sex, or other adult topics. "Our characters act silly, even totally ridiculous at times, and most of our jokes don't come out of pop cultural references," he says. "It seems like we're aiming at a child audience, but everyone can laugh at the basic human traits that are funny. It's playful, the humor is playful, the world is playful. You can kind of let go."[39] Hillenburg says that the core premise of the show is that innocence prevails. "Originally I wanted the show to focus on this innocent, optimistic, overly enthusiastic, sometimes odd and even magical character (SpongeBob) living this nautical fantasy world. I think we've pretty much stayed on course. The key has been finding stories where either SpongeBob prevails innocently or where his innocence causes a conflict for himself,"[40] he says. The result has been a show that is funny while still retaining the silliness of childhood.

> "It seems like we're aiming at a child audience, but everyone can laugh at the basic human traits that are funny. It's playful, the humor is playful, the world is playful. You can kind of let go."[39]
>
> —Stephen Hillenburg.

Pitching the Idea to Nickelodeon

Eventually, Hillenburg thought the idea was ready to pitch to executives at Nickelodeon. He used all of his skills to create an original presentation that would sell executives on his idea for the show. For the pitch, he brought in an aquarium, artwork, and sculpted characters that explained the show's story line. He also created a theme song for the proposed idea, which he played on a ukulele and sang.

Eric Coleman was a vice president of animation development and production at Nickelodeon from 1992 to 2008 and was present for Hillenburg's presentation. He remembers Hillenburg coming in dressed in a Hawaiian shirt that day. "He had an aquarium with little versions of the characters inside," Coleman says. "He had rigged up a seashell that, when you held it up to your ear, played Hawaiian music instead of ocean sounds." Coleman says that while Hillenburg's presentation was fun, the potential of his idea sold Nickelodeon executives on SpongeBob. "The show he pitched had art that really caught our eye and a character with such a funny personality. He was able to convey the sense of the show overall that just really seemed fun. In a pitch meeting like that, the goal is not for it to seem like [the] greatest thing ever. The goal is for it to seem interesting enough to develop it further,"[41] Coleman says.

Nickelodeon executives loved Hillenburg's idea and gave him a green light to move forward and develop a pilot for the show. "It was all there from the very first pitch,"[42] remembers Coleman. Hillenburg had already created most of the details for his underwater world. He knew his characters' core personality traits, the relationships between characters, and the details of their lives and world. Coleman recalls:

> So as we moved forward in making the pilot and then picking up the series, it was just a matter of letting out the stories that Steve already had in his head. He didn't necessarily have every story already worked out, but he had the relationships worked out. And when you look at the early episodes, they establish the relationships very clearly. And they not only establish the relationships, but they establish a simplicity in the storytelling, a variety in visual techniques.[43]

Eventually, Nickelodeon executives picked up the show as a series, and Hillenburg and his team got to work creating episodes.

CHAPTER THREE

The Success of *SpongeBob SquarePants*

Creating an episode of *SpongeBob SquarePants* is a well-planned and meticulous process. Many people are involved in the show's production, from the initial story idea to the finished twenty-two-minute episode. It is also a time-consuming process, with an eleven-minute story segment taking about ten to eleven months to create. Hillenburg was the showrunner, the person responsible for the day-to-day operations of the cartoon series. He was responsible for all of the creative aspects of the show and participated in developing story lines and writing scripts. In addition, Hillenburg oversaw the hiring of writers and other crew members, reviewed the show's budgets, and met with network bosses when needed.

To begin developing an episode, Hillenburg and the show's writers come up with story ideas. Because almost every episode of the cartoon show is split into two eleven-minute segments, most shows require two separate ideas. "It's very challenging to come up with 40 different stories per season. Each show features two stories. In the four seasons the show has been running, that adds up to 160 different stories," says story editor Steven Banks. "One of the things that makes 'SpongeBob' work so well is the fact that there are not too many characters to keep track of. However, that is also what makes creating new stories all the time more difficult."[44]

Many episode ideas are based on common childhood experiences. For example, in the episode titled "Sailor Mouth," SpongeBob learns a curse word, something many children can identify with. Some episode ideas come from the writers' own childhood experiences. In "Patrick's

Secret Box," SpongeBob wants to know what is in the box. The idea for the episode was based on a secret box that staffer Derek Drymon had as a child.

Overall the writers say that they try to keep the episodes simple. They look for humor in simple situations, building an entire episode around one silly situation. In one episode the writers built the story around the idea that SpongeBob and Patrick both had candy bars. Patrick forgot that he ate his and thinks that SpongeBob has stolen his candy. Hillenburg says, "The humor should always come from character. The ideas come from everywhere and anyone. Things like childhood memories. When developing stories we often play non-linear thinking exercises (like pulling words out of a hat and writing a situation inspired by the word). Ultimately the ideas that stick are the ones that consistently make everyone laugh."[45]

Once the writers have an idea, they develop story outlines and submit them to Nickelodeon for approval. Once the premise is approved, storyboard directors take over. Near the beginning Hillenburg decided that *SpongeBob SquarePants* would be a storyboard-driven, instead of a script-driven, series. Artists take a story outline and fill it with sight gags, dialogue, action, and jokes. A team of two storyboard artists works on each SpongeBob cartoon. It takes the team about two weeks to write all the dialogue and jokes. During that time Hillenburg and the show's other creative directors review the team's work and give suggestions. Over the next several weeks, the storyboard team repeats the process, designs each character's appearance, places them in the scenes, and fills in scene backgrounds. Sherm Cohen, a writer, storyboard artist, and director on the show from 1999 to 2005, explains:

> "One of the things that makes 'SpongeBob' work so well is the fact that there are not too many characters to keep track of. However, that is also what makes creating new stories all the time more difficult."[44]
>
> —Steven Banks, story editor.

> For each *SpongeBob* episode, the storyboard team starts with a bare-bones story premise that covers the basics like the setup, the complication, and the ending. The board artists are expected to flesh it all out and add lots of gags and silliness. We

would spend the first week of our six-week rotation sketching and scribbling out a very rough board on Post-It notes and on storyboard paper, fleshing out the story using sketches and handwritten notes, which we pin up on the wall so we can see how the whole thing works together.[46]

At this point, the voice actors record the characters' voices for the episode. The voice actors typically record together in the studio as an ensemble. Directors make sure that the actors' voice performances match up to the storyboard actions.

After the dialogue is recorded, the team creates a rough video storyboard with movement and sound. This helps the team make sure the jokes are timed right and the story is clear. Then the art director and his team go through the storyboards creating color palettes for the characters. Background designers create the settings for each scene. A background artist may spend several days on a single drawing that only appears in the cartoon for a few seconds.

Once the storyboards are completed and approved by Hillenburg and the show's creative directors, they are sent overseas to a studio in Korea, where a crew draws the animation. The Korean crew uses the storyboard as a template to produce the animations. During the first season, animators used traditional cel animation. Every cel was hand painted in a time-consuming process. In later seasons the show used digital ink and paint animation. This process uses traditional ink and paint to draw the animations, but the drawings are then scanned into a computer, where they are colored and processed using a software package that compiles them onto digital video instead of film.

When the animation is finished, it returns to the team in the United States. At this point, the production team edits the episode and adds music to the animation. Finally complete, the episode is ready to air on television.

Television Premiere

The first episode of *SpongeBob SquarePants* premiered on Nickelodeon in 1999. The show quickly became a hit with kids, who loved its humor and characters. Every week kids tuned in to see what crazy situation SpongeBob had gotten himself into. At first the show

SpongeBob *episodes are based on simple stories taken from real childhood experiences such as two boys eating candy bars. In one episode, SpongeBob and Patrick each had candy bars, but Patrick forgot that he ate his and thought SpongeBob stole it.*

aired on Saturday mornings. According to Tom Kenny, the voice of SpongeBob, the show first hooked kids and over time began to draw in entire families. "It started out with kids, then their older siblings started to like it. Then parents started to catch what's going on and were surprised and gratified to see a show that was funny and for all ages, with no dirty stuff,"[47] Kenny says.

During its second season, which began in February 2000, *SpongeBob SquarePants* thrived. Within a year of its debut, the show moved past Nickelodeon's hit cartoon series *Rugrats* to become the network's highest-rated show of all time. In 2001 Nickelodeon moved *SpongeBob SquarePants* to 8:00 p.m. on Monday through Friday

SpongeBob Games

SpongeBob has also made the leap to apps and video games. Released in 2013, the "SpongeBob Moves In" app lets fans move into SpongeBob's pineapple house, get a job at the Krusty Krab, and experience life in Bikini Bottom. The app was ranked number one on the iTunes charts for twelve weeks. SpongeBob video games have been similarly successful. Launched in 2014, the *SpongeBob: You're Fired!* game has been strong internationally. According to Ron Johnson, executive vice president of consumer products at Viacom International Media Networks, SpongeBob apps and games are a global business that keeps expanding.

nights. The show attracted more than 60 million viewers a month. About one-third of its viewers were adults between ages eighteen and forty-nine.

Critic Reception

Many critics received the show favorably. Terry Kelleher from *People* magazine claimed the cartoon was one of his favorite shows. He said that Hillenburg "has made it a continuing comic delight, wildly imaginative yet never too clever for its own good."[48] Veronica Chambers, a *Newsweek* critic, reviewed the show and said that the "best thing about the show is how Hillenburg's passion for the sea comes shining through."[49] The verdict was in. Hillenburg's *SpongeBob SquarePants* was a hit.

Not everyone, however, was enthralled with the little yellow sponge. Emily Ashby, a TV reviewer at Common Sense Media, an organization that provides education and advocates for safe technology and media for children, warned that the cartoon might confuse kids who have difficulty separating fantasy and reality. She pointed out that the characters often engaged in name-calling, mocking, and fantasy violence. Ashby also stated that the characters' annoying behaviors and silliness sometimes overpowered any positive messages about friendship and self-respect.

Worldwide Phenomenon

In the years since the show first premiered in 1999, *SpongeBob SquarePants* transformed from a silly Saturday morning children's television show to a worldwide pop culture phenomenon. The show's success has amazed many people, including Hillenburg himself. "I never imagined working on the show to this date and this long," he said in an interview in 2009 for the show's tenth anniversary. "It never was possible to conceive that. . . . I really figured we might get a season and a cult following, and that might be it."[50]

Since the show's launch, millions of people have watched the silly yellow sponge's adventures under the sea. *SpongeBob SquarePants* has become the most-watched animated program with kids aged two to eleven for more than twelve consecutive years, according to a 2013 Nickelodeon press release. In recent years the show has averaged more than 100 million total viewers every quarter across all Nickelodeon networks.

Hillenburg's success with *SpongeBob SquarePants* can be traced to his ability to create a character and show that appeal to people of all ages, backgrounds, and nationalities. The show entertains preschoolers, kids, teens, college students, and adults. Kids enjoy the show's silly, slapstick humor, while adults chuckle over its dry wit. Hillenburg says that the show's large adult following does not surprise him. "Since we write things that make us laugh one could assume other adults would also find the show amusing. We definitely don't pander to kids . . . but we also try not to write over their heads,"[51] he explains. Steven Banks, one of the show's writers, says that they do not aim to write kid material. "We are trying to make a show that we would laugh at when we watch," says Banks. "If you could say 10 million 8-year-olds would love this, every show would be a hit—and that doesn't happen. So it's what we think is funny."[52]

SpongeBob's humor has made him loved around the world. The show airs in more than 170 countries and is translated into more than thirty-five languages. It is distributed worldwide by Viacom Media Networks, the American mass media company that owns the Nickelodeon television network. "We launched the series internationally soon after it debuted in the U.S. and it has been a hit since day one," says Ron Johnson, executive vice president of consumer products at

Viacom International Media Networks. "The show drives ratings in every market, and ranks as a top 10 program in Australia, Brazil, Canada, Germany, Spain, India, Italy, Mexico, Poland, Russia, the U.K. and South Africa."[53]

In Japan young people have flocked to the square yellow sponge. *SpongeBob SquarePants* attracts nearly 1.9 million Japanese households to his daily television show. "We were told for a long time that SpongeBob just was a character that wouldn't work in Japan," says Viacom International Japan Vice President Ed Wells. "But if you look everywhere around the world, SpongeBob has really become a huge phenomenon."[54]

SpongeBob waves at fans taking part in an event for children in Japan. Nearly 1.9 million Japanese households watch SpongeBob SquarePants *on television every day.*

Awards and Honors

Hillenburg's *SpongeBob SquarePants* has been nominated for and won several awards and honors. In 2002 the show received its first Emmy nomination for outstanding children's program. Emmy Awards recognize excellence in the television industry. Since then the show has received numerous daytime and prime-time Emmy nominations, winning a Daytime Emmy Award in 2010 for Outstanding Special Class Animated Program and another Daytime Emmy Award in 2014 for Outstanding Sound Editing—Animation.

Over the years, *SpongeBob SquarePants* has been nominated for many other awards, including Annie Awards, BAFTA Children's Awards, ASCAP Film & Television Music Awards, Kids' Choice Awards, Teen Choice Awards, and Television Critics Association Awards. It has won several of these awards. In 2002 the show won the Television Critics Association Award for Outstanding Achievement in Children's Programming.

Hillenburg has also been singled out for his work on *SpongeBob SquarePants*. In 2001 Heal the Bay, a nonprofit environmental public interest group in Southern California, paid tribute to Hillenburg by awarding him the group's highest honor, the Walk the Talk Award. The group selected Hillenburg to receive this award for his work elevating marine life awareness through *SpongeBob SquarePants*. In 2002 the National Cartoonists Society honored Hillenburg with a Television Animation Award. That same year Hillenburg received the Statue Award in film from the Princess Grace Foundation-USA.

A Multibillion Dollar Sponge

The worldwide appeal and success of *SpongeBob SquarePants* has launched the show and its characters into a multibillion-dollar retail property for Nickelodeon. In 2001 SpongeBob starred in his first "Got Milk?" ad. Over the next few years as the cartoon's popularity skyrocketed, a licensing blitz took off. Nickelodeon, which owns the SpongeBob trademark, partnered with companies like Burger King, Target, and Hasbro to license SpongeBob's image to appear on T-shirts, posters, games, books, dolls, MP3 players, and electronics. Fans flocked to stores to purchase their own piece of SpongeBob's eternal optimism. "[The] staying power of the property is second to none," says Cindy Syracuse, senior director of cultural marketing for Burger King. "The most striking example of its popularity occurred in 2004, when our oversized SpongeBob inflatables were stolen off of the rooftops of numerous restaurants nationwide. The 'Spongenappings' ignited an inflatable frenzy among fans and the media."[55]

Since its debut *SpongeBob SquarePants* has become the most widely distributed intellectual property in Viacom's history. To date, it has rung up more than $13 billion in global consumer product sales. It has more than seven hundred license partners worldwide. "In this time frame, nothing has done this well,"[56] says Pam Kaufman, chief marketing officer and president of consumer products at Nickelodeon.

Mark Kingston is the general manager and senior vice president for Nickelodeon & Viacom Consumer Products Europe, Middle East, Africa, and Australia. During a presentation at a 2013 London brand licensing event, he compared SpongeBob to other iconic characters such as Mickey Mouse, Bugs Bunny, and Kermit the Frog. "Every half second, someone on the planet is interacting with SpongeBob,"[57] he said.

> "Every half second, someone on the planet is interacting with SpongeBob."[57]
>
> —Mark Kingston, general manager and senior vice president for Nickelodeon & Viacom Consumer Products Europe, Middle East, Africa and Australia.

Fifteen years after the show first aired on television, the SpongeBob franchise remains a powerhouse brand, and it continues to expand its reach through new opportunities. "We're working on a big program with Toys 'R' Us and have new lines debuting from Just Play, Imaginext and MEGA Bloks this year," said Kaufman in 2014. "We have 60 new licensees on board across toy, costume, and apparel, publishing and outdoor categories."[58]

Macy's Holiday Ambassador

In 2014 Macy's chose SpongeBob SquarePants to serve as the Macy's Holiday Ambassador. As part of the program, Macy's featured an exclusive SpongeBob talking plush doll that re-creates SpongeBob's laugh and funny quotes in more than six hundred Macy's stores, along with Patrick and Plankton finger puppets. SpongeBob also made his

Hasbro unveils a new version of the SpongeBob SquarePants edition of the popular Monopoly game. Devoted fans have bought everything from games to dolls to T-shirts to MP3 players, which all sport SpongeBob's image.

eleventh appearance as a balloon in the 2014 Macy's Thanksgiving Day Parade in New York City. His image was featured on holiday posters and signs in Macy's stores around the country. Several stores also planned SpongeBob in-store events. "*SpongeBob SquarePants* has experienced many iconic moments over the last 15 years, and we are honored to add Macy's coveted holiday ambassadorship to the list," says Kaufman. "We're really excited about the program. The holidays are a magical time of year, and who better than SpongeBob, the eternal optimist, to deck the halls with cheer this season?"[59]

At Macy's flagship store in Herald Square in New York City, shoppers received custom-designed shopping bags with SpongeBob's

Voice Talent

Each episode of *SpongeBob SquarePants* features the talents of several voice actors. With the help of a casting director, Stephen Hillenburg chose the actors and actresses who would become the voices of SpongeBob's characters. Before casting them, Hillenburg says that he had a rough idea in his head what the voices should sound like. He though SpongeBob should have a squeaky little voice, while Squidward's voice would be more like the character Bert from *Sesame Street*. Hillenburg has also said that he purposely tried not to use the voices of well-known actors for his characters, like other cartoons have done.

In the early years Hillenburg directed a weekly voice recording session with a full cast of actors. Everyone was in the same room to record each part. Actor Tom Kenny was chosen to play the voice of SpongeBob, while Bill Fagerbakke speaks as his best friend, Patrick Star. Other regular voice actors on the show include Rodger Bumpass as Squidward Tentacles, Clancy Brown as Mr. Krabs, and Carolyn Lawrence as Sandy Cheeks. Lawrence remembers that when she first got the job of voicing Sandy, Hillenburg gave her an enormous pile of information on Texas, squirrels, and dialects. She says that his passion for the project was something she had never before seen.

image. The store also erected a cold-air inflatable at the store's entrance and devoted a window on its famous Thirty-Fourth Street side to decorate for a Bikini Bottom holiday with exclusive plush toys and other holiday decor.

Licensing Rights

Because Nickelodeon owns the licensing rights to *SpongeBob Square-Pants* and its characters, Hillenburg has had little control over which products or ad campaigns use images from the show. However, Julie Pistor of Nickelodeon says that the company respects Hillenburg's integrity and listens to his input on merchandising. One time Hillenburg spoke up when he believed a proposed use of his character was not appropriate. When Target department stores wanted to use the song "Hip to Be Square" by Huey Lewis to promote a line of Sponge-Bob movie merchandise, Hillenburg objected. He said that he never intended SpongeBob to be hip and the idea went against everything people loved about the yellow sponge. "No offense to Huey Lewis," Hillenburg says. "But the idea of SpongeBob is that he isn't hip, so the song really goes against that. What's special and funny about the character is that he's pretty unaware and dorky. And, besides, it just seemed like we didn't need to align ourselves with a really well-known pop song."[60] In response to Hillenburg's objections, Target designed a new marketing slogan—"Dare to Be Square." The new slogan better matched Hillenburg's and SpongeBob's ideals, and Hillenburg approved.

Because Nickelodeon owns the licensing rights for *SpongeBob SquarePants* and its characters, the network, not Hillenburg, has mainly profited from the licensing deals from the show. Instead, Hillenburg has been paid a producer's fee for each episode he works on. He explains:

> It is a pretty standard deal. No one is going to invest in producing a show if they don't own it. The best thing about the deal we have here is the creative freedom. They gave us a hands-off deal and let us create the show we wanted to create. That is as important to me as the money—the chance to create something I really like and do a good job at it. Nickelodeon is not a low-budget kind of place. They gave us a budget comparable to [that of] a prime time TV show. That was also very important to me.[61]

Surprised with Success

Many fans are not surprised at the success a little yellow sponge has had around the world. "I'm not surprised at all that SpongeBob is an icon for our time," said Judy McGrath, chair and CEO of MTV Networks, "Even our president [Barack Obama] mentioned him as one of his favorites. Bob is unflappable,

"I'm not surprised at all that SpongeBob is an icon for our time."[62]

—Judy McGrath, chair and CEO of MTV Networks.

uninhibited and unstoppably optimistic. The Sponge reaches across every audience we serve, so we're jumping at this opportunity to celebrate him."[62]

For Hillenburg, however, the frenzy over SpongeBob SquarePants and his friends from Bikini Bottom has been an amazing surprise. "It kind of blew me over," he says. "Just seeing all the products out there and complete strangers wearing a drawing of a character that you created. . . . It's both wonderful and strange."[63] In his wildest dreams, he never imagined that his cartoon about a little yellow sponge would be loved by millions of people around the world.

CHAPTER FOUR

New Pursuits and Controversies

After the show's third season, which aired over a three-year-period from October 2001 to October 2004, Hillenburg and his production team took a break from creating more television episodes and shifted their focus to a new challenge, a feature-length *Sponge-Bob SquarePants* film. At first Hillenburg turned down requests from Nickelodeon and Paramount Pictures to make a SpongeBob movie. For more than a year, he refused. Then, while watching *The Iron Giant* and *Toy Story* movies with his son, Hillenburg realized that he wanted to take on the challenge of a movie. "I never wanted to do a movie because I didn't think that what we wanted to say needed to be in a movie," he says. "I like the short form for animation. Then this story idea came up that lent itself to a longer format. You can't do a road trip adventure in a short form."[64]

The SpongeBob SquarePants Movie

To write the film, Hillenburg and five other writers who had worked on the television show—Paul Tibbitt, Derek Drymon, Aaron Springer, Kent Osborne, and Tim Hill—sat in a room together for three months. "It was hugely fun, although it did get kind of gamy [smelly] in there,"[65] says Osborne. Hillenburg says that taking SpongeBob from his eleven-minute story format and expanding it to a film-length adventure was a challenge. "To do a 75-minute movie about Sponge-Bob wanting to make some jellyfish jelly would be a mistake, I think," he explains. "This had to be SpongeBob in a great adventure. That's where the comedy's coming from, having these two naïve characters, SpongeBob and Patrick, a doofus and an idiot, on this incredibly dangerous heroic odyssey with all the odds against them."[66]

Despite his initial reservations, Hillenburg enjoyed the moviemaking process. "It was very exciting to be able to take more time to think about the story, the jokes and the drawings. The TV schedule is tight, and you don't always have a lot of time to work on your drawings. I think the movie's drawings are much superior than the TV show," he says. Hillenburg used hand-drawn 2-D animation in the film, even though many other cartoon feature films at the time had switched over to 3-D computer animation. "There's a lot of talk about 2-D being dead, and I hope people don't think that . . . it's all about what you're trying to say. There are many ways to tell a story, and what's unique about animation is that there are many styles with which to tell a story,"[67] he says. In addition to hand-drawn animation, the film also incorporated live-action scenes that were shot in Santa Monica, California.

Hillenburg pretends to shoot a scene from The SpongeBob SquarePants Movie, *which was released in 2004. The movie, which he produced and directed, was a financial success and got mostly positive reviews.*

Directed and produced by Hillenburg, *The SpongeBob SquarePants Movie* opened in theaters on November 19, 2004. It starred the regular SpongeBob cast, as well as guest appearances by well-known actors Scarlett Johannsson, Jeffrey Tambor, Alec Baldwin, and David Hasselhoff. In the film, Plankton devises a plan to steal King Neptune's crown and ship it to Shell City. SpongeBob and Patrick embark on a mythical hero's quest to retrieve King Neptune's stolen crown in order to save Mr. Krabs and Bikini Bottom from Neptune's wrath. Throughout the fast-paced film, SpongeBob and Patrick display their childlike humor.

The film was a financial success and earned more than $140 million worldwide on a budget of only $30 million. Critics also received the film with generally positive reviews. Film critic Roger Ebert gave the movie three out of four stars, saying, "This is the 'Good Burger' of animation, plopping us down inside a fast-food war being fought by sponges, starfish, crabs, tiny plankton and mighty King Neptune.... All of this happens in jolly animation with bright colors and is ever so much more entertaining than you are probably imagining."[68]

> "There are many ways to tell a story, and what's unique about animation is that there are many styles with which to tell a story."[67]
>
> —*SpongeBob SquarePants* creator Stephen Hillenburg.

Controversies and Change

Although the *SpongeBob SquarePants* cartoon and movie enjoyed worldwide success, attracting millions of viewers and selling licensed products, it was not always smooth sailing for the show and its creator. Over the years, the show has encountered some controversy. And after *The SpongeBob SquarePants Movie*, Hillenburg decided that changes were ahead for the residents of Bikini Bottom.

SpongeBob's Sexuality

Although Hillenburg intended for *SpongeBob SquarePants* to be an innocent, childlike character, some people believe that the show incorporates gender and sexuality themes. From the early days of the show, rumors surfaced that SpongeBob was gay. Those who believed that the character had homosexual tendencies pointed to his relationship with best friend Patrick Star, with whom he often holds hands. The SpongeBob character grew in popularity with gay men. When asked, Hillenburg denied that SpongeBob was gay, saying that sexual orientation had nothing to do with the show.

Still, rumors over SpongeBob's sexual orientation persisted. Critics claimed that some episodes of the show featured gender and sexuality themes. In some episodes SpongeBob and his friends cross-dress. In an episode titled "That's No Lady," Patrick Star puts on women's clothing in order to conceal his identity because he believes that he is in danger. He becomes "Patricia," wearing lipstick, blonde ponytails, and a miniskirt. In other episodes SpongeBob himself has dressed in feminine clothing and has worn lipstick.

In an episode titled "Rock-a-Bye Bivalve," SpongeBob and Patrick adopt a baby scallop. SpongeBob assumes the maternal role, wearing hair curlers while he cleans, irons, and takes care of the baby scallop. Patrick assumes the masculine role and becomes the little family's breadwinner. By using two males as parents, some people say the show challenges societal norms.

In 2005 the controversy over SpongeBob's sexuality reignited when SpongeBob appeared with several other popular cartoon characters in a video that promoted tolerance and understanding. The video was produced by Nile Rodgers, the founder of the We Are Family Foundation, a nonprofit organization that promotes respect, understanding, and cultural diversity. The video features children's characters dancing and singing to a version of Sister Sledge's 1979 hit song "We Are Family." Rodgers, who wrote the song, says that he intended it to teach children about cooperation and unity.

The video sparked controversy when several conservative groups asserted that it promoted a homosexual lifestyle. The Mississippi-based American Family Association spoke out against the video. "On the surface, the project may appear to be a worthwhile attempt to foster greater understanding of cultural differences,"[69] wrote Ed Vitagliano, an editor with the American Family Association's monthly journal. Yet Vitagliano claimed that the video celebrated homosexuality.

SpongeBob landed in the middle of the controversy when James Dobson, the founder of the conservative Christian group Focus on

Cognitive Controversy

In 2011 a research report in the journal *Pediatrics* led parents to ask if watching SpongeBob was bad for their kids. In the study, researchers from the University of Virginia report that four-year-olds who had just watched the fast-paced *SpongeBob SquarePants* cartoon performed worse on attention tests and problem solving than children who watched a slower-paced education program or spent time drawing. The researchers tested sixty children, randomly assigning them into three groups. The first group watched nine minutes of SpongeBob. The second group watched nine minutes of the slower-paced cartoon, while the third group spent the nine minutes drawing on paper. Immediately after the children watched the cartoons, researchers tested them by giving them tasks that required following instructions, reversing the order of numbers, and resisting treats. The tests were designed to assess the children's brain's executive function, which controls attention, working memory, problem solving, and delay of gratification. The researchers report that the children who watched SpongeBob performed at half the capacity of those who watched the educational program or drew. The researchers concluded that the effect was not limited to SpongeBob cartoons, but occurred with other fast-paced cartoons as well. They suspect that the child's brain is working so hard to register everything in a fast-paced cartoon that it gets tired afterward.

Nickelodeon officials dismissed the study, saying that the preschool children tested were not SpongeBob's target audience of six- to eleven-year-olds. In addition, they questioned if the small number of children tested affected the results.

the Family, singled out the yellow sponge cartoon at a black-tie dinner in Washington, DC. Dobson told the guests at the dinner that SpongeBob's creators had put him in a pro-homosexual video. Dobson objected to the video's creators plan to mail the video to thousands of elementary schools to promote a tolerance pledge, because he believed the pledge included tolerance for differences in sexual identity. "We see the video as an insidious means by which the organisation is manipulating and potentially brainwashing kids,"[70] said Paul Batura, a spokesperson for Focus on the Family, in 2005. Rodgers, the video's creator, considers the attacks on the video and SpongeBob to be unfounded. "Focusing on SpongeBob is almost as ludicrous as focusing on the 'sexual identity' reference in the tolerance pledge,"[71] he says.

Hillenburg and those who work with him on the show insist that SpongeBob is not gay, even though he holds hands with his best friend, Patrick. In fact, Hillenburg says that the allegations about SpongeBob and Patrick's sexuality are ridiculous and that the cartoon is simply intended to be fun and to entertain. Hillenburg said in an interview in 2005, "We never intended them to be gay. I consider them to be almost asexual. We're just trying to be funny and this has got nothing to do with the show."[72]

James Dobson, founder of the conservative Christian group Focus on the Family, claimed that SpongeBob was being used to brainwash children on the subject of homosexuality. Hillenburg and Nickelodeon have denied any hidden agenda in the show or its characters.

Eric Coleman, vice president of animation development and production at Nickelodeon from 1992 to 2008, says that the idea of Hillenburg using SpongeBob to promote a hidden, pro-homosexual agenda is laughable. Coleman explains:

> I was not very concerned because I know Steve so well. I know what he thinks of the character, and I know his sense of humor. I know that he was not intending any kind of subversive undertone to the show. He is not the type of artist or writer who is trying to sneak in inappropriate double entendres or adult humor. And that's one of the things I admired about him: how pure and innocent that show is, yet how it manages to [be] fresh and irreverent in places while still being heartfelt and sincere.[73]

Lawsuit Alleges SpongeBob Was Stolen

Just as one controversy died down, another appeared in 2007 when Troy Walker, a cartoonist, claimed that Hillenburg stole his idea when creating *SpongeBob SquarePants*. In 1991 Walker created a comic strip about an unemployed cartoon sponge. His main character, Bob Spongee, had eyes, legs, and arms. He lived on Apple Street with his wife, Linda, and daughter, Bubbles. To promote his cartoon, Walker produced one thousand yellow sponge dolls with drawn-on faces. He sold the dolls in flea markets and through the mail.

When Walker watched *SpongeBob SquarePants* on Nickelodeon, he says he immediately noticed many similarities between the show and his cartoon. "They took all of it," Walker said in 2007. "I sold the Bob Spongees all throughout Northern California. It obviously fell into the hands of one of the producers of the show. It's a clear pattern of duplication."[74]

"He is not the type of artist or writer who is trying to sneak in inappropriate double entendres or adult humor. And that's one of the things I admired about him: how pure and innocent that show is."[73]

—Eric Coleman, vice president of animation development and production at Nickelodeon from 1992 to 2008.

In 2007 Walker filed a lawsuit in US District Court in San Francisco against Nickelodeon, Viacom, Paramount Studios, and Hillenburg. He alleged that the defendants used his idea without permission. In his lawsuit Walker demanded $1.6 billion in damages. In his complaint, Walker detailed his original concept of Bob Spongee—he drew a nose and mouth on a kitchen sponge and added plastic eyes. He had also drawn a small comic strip with the doll that said, "Sponge for hire! Meet Bob Spongee, The Unemployed Sponge." Walker points to an episode of *SpongeBob SquarePants* from 2004 in which SpongeBob says "Sponge for hire!" as proof that his idea was stolen. "It is more than ironic that two working-class sponges are named Bob," Walker says in his complaint. "Both characters are unemployed. Both characters live in a house concept."[75]

Although Hillenburg did not comment on the lawsuit, a representative from Nickelodeon stated that Walker's claim was baseless. Attorneys for Viacom responded to Walker's complaint and wrote in court documents that SpongeBob was not substantially similar to Walker's Bob Spongee. In 2008 U.S. District Court judge Susan Illston ruled against Walker. She dismissed his copyright infringement claim, writing in her decision that Walker had failed to prove that his 1991 comic strip was the basis of Nickelodeon's *SpongeBob SquarePants* cartoon show.

Too Sexy

In 2009 SpongeBob again came under fire from critics when the cartoon character starred in a Burger King commercial. The ad featured Burger King's King character singing a remix of Sir Mix-A-Lot's 1990s hit song "Baby Got Back." In the commercial the song's lyrics are changed to "I like square butts and I cannot lie."[76] The commercial also uses images of SpongeBob dancing, along with women shaking their backsides.

The Campaign for a Commercial-Free Childhood (CCFC) objected to the ad and claimed it was too sexy for a children's cartoon character. It started a campaign that demanded Nickelodeon and Burger King stop showing the ad for *SpongeBob SquarePants* Kids Meals. "It's bad enough when companies use a beloved media character like SpongeBob to promote junk food to children, but it's utterly reprehensible when that character simultaneously promotes objectified, sexualized images of women,"[77] says CCFC director Susan Linn, a psychologist at the Judge Baker Children's Center. Although Burger King continued to air the ad, its restaurant owners complained that the awkward use of SpongeBob ultimately alienated customers and failed to increase Burger King's sales.

Stepping Down

After completing *The SpongeBob SquarePants Movie* in 2004, Hillenburg was concerned that the show had run its course. Nickelodeon, however, still wanted new episodes of its money-making property. So Hillenburg decided it was time for him to take a step back. He resigned as the showrunner and appointed Paul Tibbitt, who had previously served as the show's supervising producer, writer, director, and storyboard artist, as the new showrunner.

Although he was no longer writing or running the show on a day-to-day basis, Hillenburg took an executive producer role with the show. He remained involved in reviewing episodes and making suggestions to the staff. "It reached a point where I felt I'd contributed a lot and said what I wanted to say. At that point, the show needed new blood and so I selected Paul [Tibbitt] to produce," Hillenburg says. "I totally trusted him. I always enjoyed the way he captured the SpongeBob character's sense of humor. And as a writer, you have to move on—I'm developing new projects."[78]

> "It reached a point where I felt I'd contributed a lot and said what I wanted to say. At that point, the show needed new blood and so I selected Paul [Tibbitt] to produce."[78]
>
> —*SpongeBob SquarePants* creator Stephen Hillenburg.

New Pursuits

After stepping down as showrunner, Hillenburg now had more time to pursue other interests. He created a short film titled *Hollywood Blvd, USA* that was eventually released in 2014. For the film, he videotaped people on Hollywood Boulevard and created animations of how they walked.

A Fungi Named SpongeBob

Scientists have named a newly discovered fungus *Spongiforma squarepantsii,* after the beloved yellow cartoon sponge. The fungus is bright orange, full of holes, and looks like a sponge. It lives in rainforests on the tropical island of Borneo. Not only is the fungus named after a sponge, it also acts like one. When it is wet and moist, water can be wrung out of it and the fungus will spring back to its original size and shape like a sponge.

The genus name, *Spongiforma*, refers to the close resemblance the fungus has to a sea sponge. The name *squarepantsii* is a Latin version of "SquarePants." At first some people rejected the cartoon name as too silly. But the scientists who codiscovered the fungus—Dennis Desjardin, a professor of ecology and evolution at San Francisco State University; Kabir Peay, an assistant professor of plant pathology at the University of Minnesota; and Thomas Bruns, a professor of ecology and evolution at the University of California at Berkeley—insisted that they had the right to name it whatever they wanted.

In total, Hillenburg says the film runs for only a couple of minutes. He has entered it in several film festivals.

In February 2011 Hillenburg announced the release of a thirty-two-page comic book series, *SpongeBob Comics*, based on the television show and published by United Plankton Pictures, a television and film production company formed by Hillenburg in 1998. In addition to the comic book series, United Plankton Pictures produces the *SpongeBob SquarePants* television series, movies, and related media in association with Nickelodeon Animation Studios.

SpongeBob Comics is the first time the characters from Bikini Bottom have appeared in their own comic book in the United States. To make the comic, Hillenburg gathered a group of comic book writers and artists. Each issue features thirty-two pages of feature-length stories, shorts, and fun pages, aimed at fans of all ages. "I'm hoping that fans will enjoy finally having a 'SpongeBob' comic book from me," says Hillenburg. "All the stories will be original and always true to the humor, characters, and universe of the 'SpongeBob SquarePants' series."[79]

The comic book was first published bimonthly, then moved to a monthly issue in 2012. Upon reading the comic's debut issue, Chad Nevett of Comic Book Resources wrote, "For a debut issue, 'SpongeBob Comics' is effective at capturing the tone of the show and allowing the creators to present their own takes on the characters at times. It suffers sometimes from not being able to rely on the strengths of animation and, hopefully, will take advantage of the things that comics can do that animation can't, adapting its style to this medium more."[80]

Private Time

Outside of *SpongeBob SquarePants*, Hillenburg has built a life in Southern California with his wife and son. When he is not working, he reportedly still enjoys the ocean and spending time surfing, snorkeling, and scuba diving. He also likes to play guitar, saying, "At home I've been jamming with my 14-year-old son. He plays drums and I play guitar—horribly. It's a great way to bond with each other."[81]

Still an artist, Hillenburg enjoys painting in his spare time. In a 2013 interview, he talked about his painting:

> I paint surreal seascapes. Sometimes they are based on something that's happened, like when I was camping on the coast in Baja on a surf trip awhile ago. In the middle of the night I saw this glow outside the tent. There was a full moon over the water and it was shining into this fog bank. It created a complete rainbow—only it was a moonbow. So for one of the paintings I painted a moonbow over the water. I haven't sold any of my paintings. I don't know. There's something personal about it. I'm holding on to them right now. Maybe I'll have a show one of these days.[82]

According to friends, Hillenburg is a very private man. He rarely grants interviews and prefers to keep his personal life private. "He never intended for the show to be successful on this level," says Julie Pistor, senior vice president of Nickelodeon Movies. "I think that has really overwhelmed him. He's very shy. He doesn't want people to know about his life or family. He's just a really funny, down-to-earth guy with a dry sense of humor who puts his family first and keeps us on our toes in keeping our corporate integrity."[83]

2015 Movie Sequel

For several years Nickelodeon and Paramount executives wanted to bring SpongeBob back to the big screen. They first, however, had to convince Hillenburg and Paul Tibbett, the television series' show-runner, that it was a good idea. In a 2009 interview, Tibbett said that he doubted another movie would be made. "I think that they are talking about doing that, but I haven't signed up for anything. We just feel like we've told so many stories, and SpongeBob exists so well in this short 11-minute form. It is a huge challenge, and was a huge challenge, to make a 75-minute movie. I wouldn't say no, but I don't know if there will be another one,"[84] he said.

Eventually, Tibbett and Hillenburg agreed to create a new feature-length SpongeBob film. In 2012 executives from Viacom's Paramount Pictures unit and Nickelodeon announced that there would be a new *SpongeBob SquarePants* movie. "SpongeBob is as vigorous as ever and firmly fits into that slate of franchise brands," says Philippe Dauman, Viacom's chief executive. Dauman says that the new movie will help reignite interest in the television series. He also believes that the movie will do better overseas than the 2004 film, because of Nickelodeon's increased global reach. "This will continue to propel SpongeBob internationally,"[85] he says.

Hillenburg has been working as the executive producer on the new SpongeBob movie as well as assisting director Tibbitt and his team with writing the new script. The new film, titled *The SpongeBob Movie: Sponge Out of Water*, was released in February 2015. The movie is produced by Nickelodeon Movies and Paramount Animation. It stars voice actors from the television series: Tom Kenny as Sponge-Bob, Bill Fagerbakke as Patrick Star, Rodger Bumpass as Squidward

Hillenburg's newest film, The SpongeBob Movie: Sponge Out of Water, *was released in 2015. He says he has enjoyed working on the movie because this time he's not directing it.*

Tentacles, Clancy Brown as Mr. Krabs, and Carolyn Lawrence as Sandy Cheeks. Hillenburg says that he has enjoyed working on the new movie. "The first movie was very stressful," he admits. "But this time I'm not directing. I'm more involved with the writing and I'm an executive producer. I'm actually enjoying it."[86]

In the film, the pirate Burger-Beard steals the Krabbie Patty secret formula, putting the city of Bikini Bottom in danger. SpongeBob, Patrick, and friends embark on a quest to the surface to retrieve the recipe, fight Burger-Beard, and save their city. The film combines traditional 2-D animation, live-action footage, and computer-generated imagery that allows the characters to appear in 3-D.

Back to Bikini Bottom

When asked in a 2014 interview about his plans after the SpongeBob movie sequel, Hillenburg says that he plans to get back to work on the television series. "Actually when it wraps, I want to get back to the show. As I mentioned it is getting harder and harder to come up with stories. So Paul and I are really going to brainstorm and come up with fresh material,"[87] he says. In December 2014 Tibbett announced on Twitter that Hillenburg would be officially returning to the show in January 2015.

More than a decade after the debut of *SpongeBob SquarePants*, Hillenburg remains amazed at the success and fame his funny yellow cartoon sponge has gained around the world. He says:

> I certainly never imagined we would be making another movie and be on the air for nine seasons. When I first started in animation—the show I was working on aired for four seasons and I just imagined that would be our run too. I never imagined that this would blow up the way it did. . . . You never know what the public is going to gravitate towards. We've been really fortunate."[88]

SOURCE NOTES

Introduction: Celebrating a Worldwide Icon

1. Quoted in Daniel Bubbeo, "*SpongeBob SquarePants* Celebrates 10 Years of Nautical Nonsense," PopMatters, July 13, 2009. www.popmatters.com.

2. Quoted in Bubbeo, "*SpongeBob SquarePants* Celebrates 10 Years of Nautical Nonsense."

3. Quoted in *Los Angeles Daily News*, "Soaking in Success: How a Mild-Mannered Surfer and Marine Biologist Turned His Innocent Animated Character into a $1.5 Billion Enterprise," November 23, 2004. www.thefreelibrary.com.

4. Quoted in Bubbeo, "*SpongeBob SquarePants* Celebrates 10 Years of Nautical Nonsense."

5. Quoted in *Los Angeles Daily News*, "Soaking in Success."

6. Quoted in Bubbeo, "*SpongeBob SquarePants* Celebrates 10 Years of Nautical Nonsense."

7. Quoted in *Los Angeles Daily News*, "Soaking in Success."

Chapter One: Early Life and Career

8. Craig McClain, "Archangel with Aqua-Lung," *American Scientist*, July/August 2010. www.americanscientist.org.

9. Quoted in Myles Cochrane, "Famous Humboldt: From the Redwoods to the Limelight," *Ukiah (CA) Daily Journal*, June 28, 2011. www.ukiahdailyjournal.com.

10. Quoted in Princess Grace Foundation-USA, "Happy Birthday *SpongeBob SquarePants*," April 25, 2014. www.pgfusa.com.

11. Quoted in Elisabeth Mann, "Week Sixteen: The Art of the Pitch; A Special Evening with Stephen Hillenburg!," *USC Hench DADA Seminar Blog*, April 30, 2014. http://animationseminar spring2014.wordpress.com.

12. Quoted in Princess Grace Foundation-USA, "Happy Birthday *SpongeBob SquarePants*."

13. Quoted in Michael Cavna, "The Interview: 'SpongeBob' Creator Stephen Hillenburg," *Comic Riffs* (blog), *Washington Post*, July 14, 2009. www.washingtonpost.com.

14. Quoted in M. Night Shyamalan and Time Warner, *Current Biography Yearbook 2003*. New York: Wilson, 2003, pp. 233–37.

15. Quoted in Cavna, "The Interview."

16. Quoted in Princess Grace Foundation-USA, "SpongeBob's Dad Tells All," *PGF-USA Newsletter*, 2003. www.pgfusa.com.

17. Quoted in California Institute of the Arts, "Jules Engel Centennial Celebration Honored Legendary Animator and Founder of CalArts Animation," April 22, 2009. http://calarts.edu.

18. Quoted in Jules-Engel, "Memorable Quotes." www.jules-engel.com.

19. Quoted in Princess Grace Foundation-USA, "SpongeBob's Dad Tells All."

Chapter Two: Working at Nickelodeon

20. Quoted in Tamar Lewin, "Hey There, Dudes, the Kids Have Grabbed a Network," *New York Times*, October 21, 1990. www.nytimes.com.

21. Quoted in Lewin, "Hey There, Dudes, the Kids Have Grabbed a Network."

22. Quoted in Lewin, "Hey There, Dudes, the Kids Have Grabbed a Network."

23. Quoted in Lewin, "Hey There, Dudes, the Kids Have Grabbed a Network."

24. Quoted in *Victoria (TX) Advocate*, "Nickelodeon to Offer Cartoons," August 10, 1991. www.victoriaadvocate.com.

25. Quoted in Irene Lacher, "Birth of a Nickelodeon Nation," *Los Angeles Times*, March 26, 2000. http://articles.latimes.com.

26. Quoted in Princess Grace Foundation-USA, "Happy Birthday *SpongeBob SquarePants*."

27. Quoted in Shyamalan and Time Warner, *Current Biography Yearbook 2003*, p. 234.

28. Quoted in Tom Heintjes, "The Oral History of *SpongeBob SquarePants*," *Hogan's Alley*, September 21, 2012. http://cartoonician.com.

29. Quoted in Heintjes, "The Oral History of *SpongeBob SquarePants*."

30. Quoted in Princess Grace Foundation-USA, "Happy Birthday *SpongeBob SquarePants*."

31. Quoted in Heintjes, "The Oral History of *SpongeBob SquarePants*."

32. Quoted in *Authors and Artists for Young Adults*, "Stephen Hillenburg," vol. 53. Detroit: Gale, 2003.

33. Quoted in Linda Williams Aber, "Ultimate Guide to *SpongeBob SquarePants*," HowStuffWorks. http://lifestyle.howstuffworks.com.

34. Quoted in Heintjes, "The Oral History of *SpongeBob SquarePants*."

35. Quoted in Shyamalan and Time Warner, *Current Biography Yearbook 2003*, p. 235.

36. Quoted in Princess Grace Foundation-USA, "SpongeBob's Dad Tells All."

37. Quoted in Heintjes, "The Oral History of *SpongeBob SquarePants*."

38. Quoted in Tom Zeller, "How to Succeed Without Attitude," *New York Times*, July 21, 2002. www.nytimes.com.

39. Quoted in Kathryn Shattuck, "For Young Viewers: For This Scientist, Children Are Like, Er, Sponges," *New York Times*, July 29, 2001. www.nytimes.com.

40. Quoted in David B. Levy, "*Animondays* Interview: Stephen Hillenburg," *Animondays* (blog), February 11, 2012. http://animondays.blogspot.com.

41. Quoted in Heintjes, "The Oral History of *SpongeBob SquarePants*."

42. Quoted in Heintjes, "The Oral History of *SpongeBob SquarePants*."

43. Quoted in Heintjes, "The Oral History of *SpongeBob SquarePants*."

Chapter Three: The Success of *SpongeBob SquarePants*

44. Quoted in Aber, "Ultimate Guide to *SpongeBob SquarePants*."

45. Quoted in Levy, "*Animondays* Interview."

46. Quoted in Heintjes, "The Oral History of *SpongeBob SquarePants*."

47. Quoted in *Authors and Artists for Young Adults*, "Stephen Hillenburg."

48. Quoted in *Authors and Artists for Young Adults*, "Stephen Hillenburg."

49. Quoted in *Authors and Artists for Young Adults*, "Stephen Hillenburg."

50. Quoted in Cavna, "The Interview."

51. Quoted in Levy, "*Animondays* Interview."

52. Quoted in Neal Karlinsky and Hana Karar, "Meet the Minds Behind 'SpongeBob SquarePants,'" ABC News, March 26, 2010. http://abcnews.go.com.

53. Quoted in Barbara Sax, "*SpongeBob SquarePants* Turns 15," *License! Global*, October 1, 2014. www.licensemag.com.

54. Quoted in NBC News, "SpongeBob Winning Fans in Cute-Loving Japan," January 30, 2007. www.nbcnews.com.

55. Quoted in Andrew Hampp, "How SpongeBob Became an $8 Billion Franchise," *Advertising Age*, July 13, 2009. http://adage.com.

56. Quoted in Georg Szalai, "London Expo: Nickelodeon Touts $475 Million in Retail Sales for Relaunched 'Turtles' Franchise," *Hollywood Reporter*, October 18, 2013. www.hollywoodreporter.com.

57. Quoted in Szalai, "London Expo."

58. Quoted in Sax, "*SpongeBob SquarePants* Turns 15."

59. Quoted in Sax, "*SpongeBob SquarePants* Turns 15."

60. Quoted in *Los Angeles Daily News*, "Soaking in Success."

61. Quoted in Shyamalan and Time Warner, *Current Biography Yearbook 2003*, p. 237.

62. Quoted in Hampp, "How SpongeBob Became an $8 Billion Franchise."

63. Quoted in Shyamalan and Time Warner, *Current Biography Yearbook 2003*, p. 236.

Chapter Four: New Pursuits and Controversies

64. Quoted in Barry Koltnow, "SpongeBob Creator Is Soaking Up Success," *East Valley (AZ) Tribune*, November 14, 2004. www.eastvalleytribune.com.

65. Quoted in David Edelstein, "He Lives in a Pineapple, but Then What?," *New York Times*, November 7, 2004. www.nytimes.com.

66. Quoted in Edelstein, "He Lives in a Pineapple, but Then What?"

67. Quoted in Koltnow, "SpongeBob Creator Is Soaking Up Success."

68. Roger Ebert, "*The SpongeBob SquarePants Movie*," RogerEbert.com, November 18, 2004. www.rogerebert.com.

69. Quoted in Matt Sayles, "SpongeBob, Muppets, Sister Sledge Writer Suffer Criticism," *USA Today*, January 22, 2005. http://usatoday30.usatoday.com.

70. Quoted in David D. Kirkpatrick, "Conservatives Pick Soft Target: A Cartoon Sponge," *New York Times*, January 20, 2005. www.nytimes.com.

71. Quoted in Sayles, "SpongeBob, Muppets, Sister Sledge Writer Suffer Criticism."

72. Quoted in *IOL News* (South Africa), "SpongeBob Isn't Gay or Straight, Creator Says," January 29, 2005. www.iol.co.za.

73. Quoted in Heintjes, "The Oral History of *SpongeBob SquarePants*."

74. Quoted in Bruce Gerstman, "Cartoonist Sues Creator of Sponge-Bob," *Lawrence (KS) Journal-World*, March 11, 2007. www2.lj world.com.

75. Quoted in Gerstman, "Cartoonist Sues Creator of SpongeBob."

76. Quoted in Campaign for a Commercial-Free Childhood, "CCFC to Nick and Burger King: SpongeBob and Sexualization Don't Mix!" April 7, 2009. www.commercialfreechildhood.org.

77. Quoted in Campaign for a Commercial-Free Childhood, "CCFC to Nick and Burger King: SpongeBob and Sexualization Don't Mix!"

78. Quoted in Cavna, "The Interview."

79. Quoted in Richard Boom, "SpongeBob Comics #1 Debuts from United Plankton Pictures," Wayback Machine, January 25, 2011. http://web.archive.org.

80. Chad Nevett, "Review: SpongeBob Comics #1," Comic Book Resources, February 12, 2011. www.comicbookresources.com.

81. Quoted in Kate Murphy, "Stephen Hillenburg," *New York Times*, June 15, 2013. www.nytimes.com.

82. Quoted in Murphy, "Stephen Hillenburg."

83. Quoted in *Los Angeles Daily News*, "Soaking in Success."

84. Quoted in Alex Fletcher, "Paul Tibbett ('SpongeBob SquarePants')," Digital Spy, April 3, 2011. www.digitalspy.com.

85. Quoted in Amy Chozick, "Return to Big Screen for SpongeBob," *Media Decoder* (blog), *New York Times*, March 4, 2012. http://me diadecoder.blogs.nytimes.com.

86. Quoted in Princess Grace Foundation-USA, "Happy Birthday *SpongeBob SquarePants*."

87. Quoted in Princess Grace Foundation-USA, "Happy Birthday *SpongeBob SquarePants*."

88. Quoted in Princess Grace Foundation-USA, "Happy Birthday *SpongeBob SquarePants*."

IMPORTANT EVENTS IN THE LIFE OF STEPHEN HILLENBURG

1961
Stephen McDannell Hillenburg is born in Fort Sill, Oklahoma.

Mid-1960s
The Hillenburg family moves to Southern California.

1984
Hillenburg graduates from Humboldt State University and takes a job with the Orange County Marine Institute.

1989
Hillenburg enrolls in a master's degree program at California Institute of the Arts (CalArts).

1991
Hillenburg creates his first short animated film, *The Green Beret*.

1992
Hillenburg graduates from CalArts and takes a job at Nickelodeon working on the animated television series, *Rocko's Modern Life*.

1996
After the cancellation of *Rocko's Modern Life*, Hillenburg begins actively developing a new underwater cartoon series.

1998
Hillenburg forms United Plankton Pictures, a television and film production company, which produces *SpongeBob SquarePants*.

1999
SpongeBob SquarePants premieres on the Nickelodeon television network.

2001
Hillenburg receives Heal the Bay's Walk the Talk Award for raising public awareness about marine life through *SpongeBob SquarePants*.

2002
SpongeBob SquarePants earns its first Emmy nomination for outstanding animated program (less than one hour). Hillenburg receives the National Cartoonists Society's Television Animation Award and the Statue Award in film from the Princess Grace Foundation-USA.

2003
SpongeBob SquarePants goes on hiatus as Hillenburg and his team work on a feature film.

2004
The SpongeBob SquarePants Movie is released, and Hillenburg steps down as the television series' showrunner.

2005
SpongeBob becomes the target of anti-gay activists after appearing in a tolerance video.

2007
SpongeBob SquarePants airs its one hundredth episode.

2009
Nickelodeon celebrates the tenth anniversary of *SpongeBob SquarePants* with fifty hours of *SpongeBob* programming.

2011
Hillenburg releases the first issues of *SpongeBob Comics*.

2014
SpongeBob serves as Macy's Holiday Ambassador.

2015
The SpongeBob Movie: Sponge Out of Water is released in February.

FOR FURTHER RESEARCH

Books

Jerry Beck, *The SpongeBob SquarePants Experience: A Deep Dive into the World of Bikini Bottom*. San Rafael, CA: Insight Editions, 2013.

Kathy Furgang, *Careers in Digital Animation*. New York: Rosen, 2013.

Richard Williams, *The Animator's Survival Kit: A Manual of Methods, Principles and Formulas for Classical, Computer, Games, Stop Motion and Internet Animators*. New York: Faber & Faber, 2012.

Internet Sources

Michael Cavna, "The Interview: 'SpongeBob' Creator Stephen Hillenburg," *Comic Riffs* (blog), *Washington Post*, July 14, 2009. www.washingtonpost.com/blogs/comic-riffs/post/the-interview-spongebob-creator-stephen-hillenburg/2010/12/20/ABCKVBG_blog.html.

Tom Heintjes, "The Oral History of *SpongeBob SquarePants*," *Hogan's Alley*, September 21, 2012. http://cartoonician.com/the-oral-history-of-spongebob-squarepants.

Neal Karlinsky and Hana Karar, "Meet the Minds Behind 'SpongeBob SquarePants,'" ABC News, March 26, 2010. http://abcnews.go.com/Nightline/inside-story-spongebob-squarepants/story?id=10210647.

David B. Levy, "*Animondays* Interview: Stephen Hillenburg," *Animondays* (blog), February 11, 2012. http://animondays.blogspot.com/2012/02/animondays-interview-stephen-hillenburg.html.

Princess Grace Foundation-USA, "Happy Birthday *SpongeBob SquarePants*," April 25, 2014. www.pgfusa.com/news/view/Happy-Birthday-SpongeBob-SquarePants.

Jenelle Riley, "Tom Kenny Finds His Voice as SpongeBob Square-Pants," Backstage, April 27, 2011. www.backstage.com/interview /tom-kenny-finds-his-voice-as-spongebob-squarepants.

VH1, *Square Roots: The Story of SpongeBob SquarePants*. www.vh1 .com/video/shows/full-episodes/square-roots-the-story-of-sponge bob-squarepants-full-episode/1614584/playlist.jhtml.

Websites

Bloop Animation (www.bloopanimation.com). Created by a work-ing animator, this website has step-by-step information and tips about the animation process.

Nickelodeon Animation Studio (http://nickanimationstudio.com). Take a look behind the scenes of the studio where many of Nickel-odeon's most popular cartoons, including *SpongeBob SquarePants*, are created.

SpongeBob SquarePants, **Nickelodeon** (www.nick.com/spongebob -squarepants). This website features games, online episodes, and oth-er special features for *SpongeBob SquarePants*.

INDEX

PICTURE CREDITS

ABOUT THE AUTHOR

Carla Mooney is the author of many books for young adults and children. She lives in Pittsburgh, Pennsylvania, with her husband and three children.